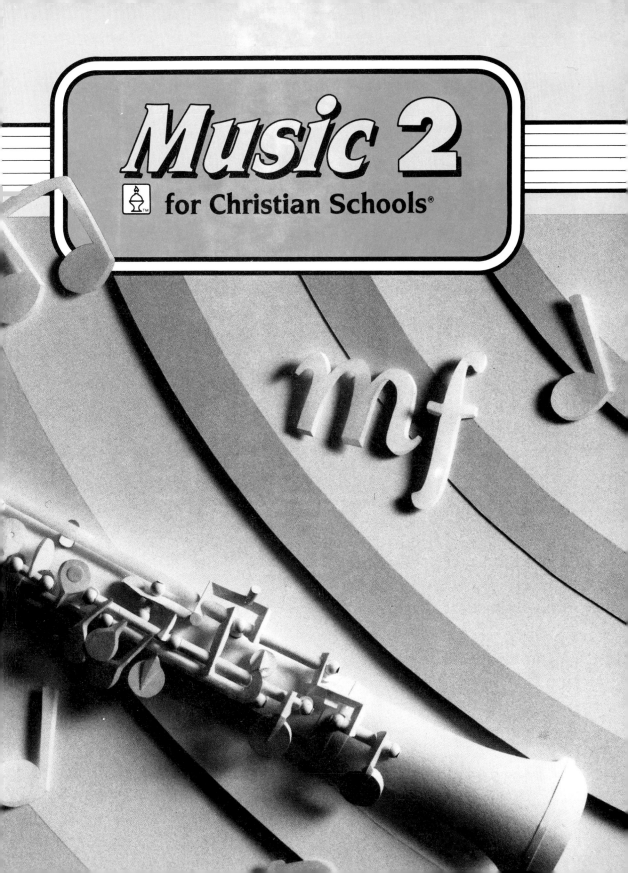

Music 2

for Christian Schools®

NOTE:
The fact that materials produced by other publishers are referred to in this volume does not constitute an endorsement by Bob Jones University Press of the content or theological position of materials produced by such publishers. The position of the Bob Jones University Press, and of the University itself, is well known. Any references and ancillary materials are listed as an aid to the student or the teacher in an attempt to maintain the accepted academic standards of the publishing industry.

MUSIC for Christian Schools® 2

Produced in cooperation with the BJU Division of Music of the School of Fine Arts, Bob Jones Elementary School, and Bob Jones Academy.

Photo credits: Cover, Unusual Films; The National Gallery, London, p. 104; Steinway and Sons, p. 113; U.S. Marine Corps, p. 16 left; Unusual Films, pp. 16 right, 17, 21, 22-23, 27, 44, 50, 110, 118; Kay Washer, p. 110.

ISBN 0-89084-385-6

©1987, 1990 Bob Jones University Press
Greenville, South Carolina 29614

20   19   18   17   16   15   14   13   12   11   10   9

Table of Contents

A fine fat frog,
Fortissimo by name,
He peered into the pond
And saw himself the same.
He croaked a catchy chorus,
"Fallumph! Fallumph! Fallett!
I seem to sing a solo, but
Reflection sings duet!"

Music Has Melody

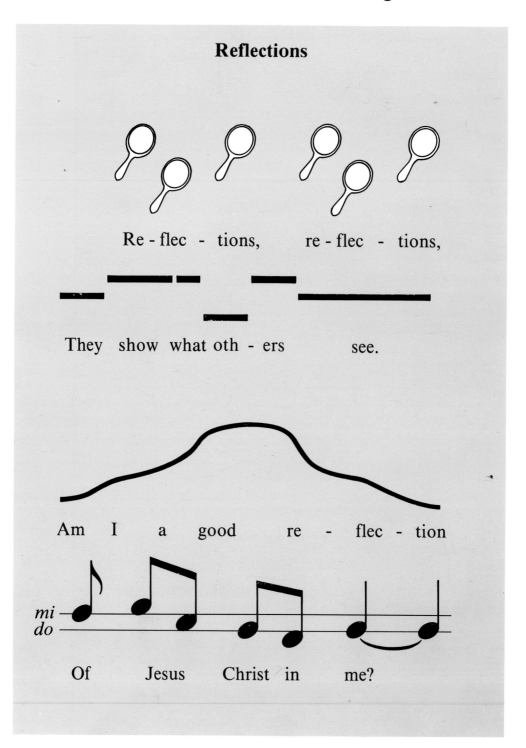

Reflections

Re - flec - tions, re - flec - tions,

They show what oth - ers see.

Am I a good re - flec - tion

mi
do

Of Jesus Christ in me?

All the Pretty Little Horses

Hushaby, don't you cry,
    Go
         to
             sleep-
                  y,
                       lit-
                            tle
                                 baby.

When you wake you shall have
    All
         the
             pret-
                  ty
                       lit-
                            tle
                               horses.

Blacks and bays, dapples and grays
    Coach
         and
             six
                  a-
                       lit-
                            tle
                               horses.

Hushaby, don't you cry,
    Go
         to
             sleep-
                  y,
                       lit-
                            tle
                               baby.

Music Has Rhythm

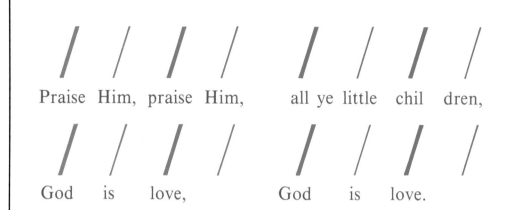

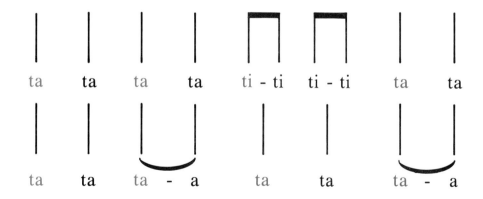

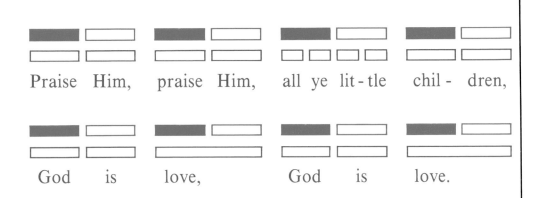

Praise Him, praise Him, all ye lit-tle chil-dren,

God is love, God is love.

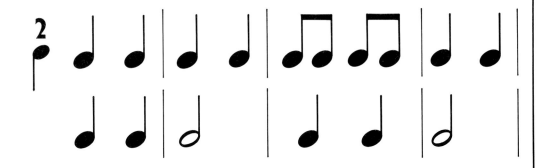

Sakura

Sakura is the Japanese word for *cherry blossoms.* The cherry tree blooms in early spring. Its beauty has inspired many poems and songs.

Sa - ku - ra,   Sa - ku - ra,

Cher - ry blos - soms in the air,

Sweet the fra - grance ev - 'ry - where,

Pet - als soft and col - ors bright,

Float - ing clouds that seem to say:

Come and see,   come and see,

Come and see the cher - ry bloom.

America the Beautiful

O, beautiful for spacious skies,
p
For amber waves of grain,

For purple mountain majesties

Above the fruited plain!

America! America!
f
God shed His grace on thee,

And crown thy good with brotherhood
mf
From sea to shining sea.

Music Moves at Different Speeds

Speed in music is called **tempo.** Music may have a fast, slow, or moderate tempo.

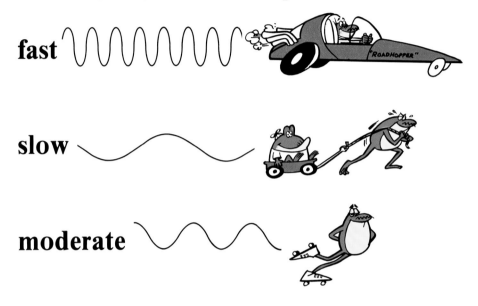

fast

slow

moderate

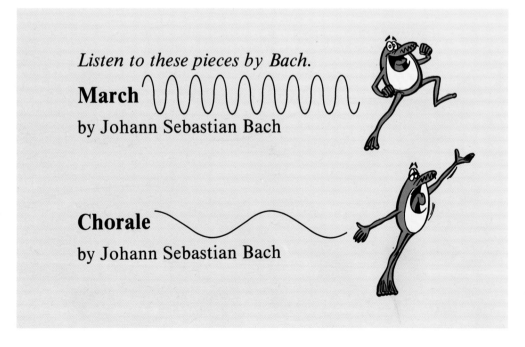

Listen to these pieces by Bach.

March

by Johann Sebastian Bach

Chorale

by Johann Sebastian Bach

Music Has Form

A piece of music may be made of many melodies. Each different melody is called a **theme.** We can draw a shape or write a letter to stand for each theme that we hear in the piece. The letters or shapes tell us the way the music is put together. We call this the music's **form.**

Musette

by Johann Sebastian Bach

The first theme begins with this short piece of the melody which we call a **motive.** We hear it four times in the theme.

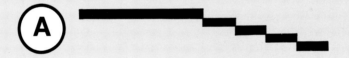

The second theme begins with this motive. It is heard only once in the theme.

AABABA or ○○□○□○ is the form of this piece.

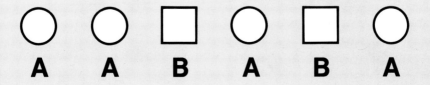

The Cuckoo

In a moderate tempo:

Oh, I went to Peter's flowing spring
Where the water's so good,
And I heard there the cuckoo
As she called from the wood.

Slowly:

Ho-lee-ah,

In a fast tempo:

Ho-lay-rah-hee-hee-ah,
Ho-lay-rah cuckoo!
Ho-lay-rah-hee-hee-ah,
Ho-lay-rah cuckoo!
Ho-lay-rah-hee-hee-ah,
Ho-lay-rah cuckoo!
Ho-lay-rah-hee-hee-ah-ho!

Yodeling is a type of singing that is done among people who live in the mountains of Austria and Switzerland. A yodeler sings quickly from low pitches to high pitches using made-up words. Often the words for the lowest pitches have an ō sound, and the words for the highest pitches have an ē sound.

Music Has Harmony

The cowboy sings a melody.
He plays the harmony on his guitar.

Billy the Kid

by Aaron Copland

1. Welcome to the frontier town! All the instruments play a greeting.

2. Violins play a quick, bright melody.

3. Several instruments play short sections of "Git Along, Little Dogies."

4. The instruments play a new tune. The trumpet, drums, and flute can be heard.

5. The entire orchestra plays "Goodbye, Old Paint."

6. Listen for drum beats as the music fades away.

Cowboys spent many lonely hours riding their horses. Often they made up songs to help pass the time, like "Goodbye, Old Paint" and "Git Along, Little Dogies." The words to the songs didn't always make sense, but the cowboys tried very hard to make them rhyme.

Goodbye, Old Paint

My foot in the stirrup, my pony won't stan';

I'm leaving Cheyenne and I'm off to Montan'.

Refrain:

Goodbye, old Paint, I'm a - leavin' Cheyenne.

Goodbye, old Paint, I'm a - leavin' Cheyenne.

I'm ridin' old Paint and I'm leadin' old Fan;

Goodbye, Little Annie, I'm off for Montan'.

Git Along, Little Dogies

*Play the Autoharp slowly
from bottom to top as you sing
the first verse.*

As I was a - walk - in' one morn - in' for plea - sure,
I spied a cow - punch - er come rid - in' a - long.
His hat was throwed back and his spurs was a - jin - gle,
And as he ap - proached he was sing - in' this song.

*Play the Autoharp with
quicker up and down strokes
as you sing the refrain.*

Refrain:

Whoo - pee ti - yi - yo, Git a - long, lit - tle do - gies,
It's your mis - for - tune and none of my own.
Whoo - pee ti - yi - yo, Git a - long, lit - tle do - gies,
You know that Mon - tan - a will be your new home.

*Play slowly on just the high
strings as you sing the second
verse.*

Ear - ly in spring - time we round up the do - gies,
Mark 'em and brand 'em and cut off their tails.
Then we all load up the old chuck wag - on,
And hitch up our hor - ses and start up the trail.

Sing the refrain again.

Music Has Many Different Sounds

The sounds of music are made by instruments. God has given every person a very special instrument. That instrument is the human voice, and no two voices sound exactly alike. God has also allowed men to invent other instruments that can make many different sounds. People today play instruments made of wood, metal, or plastic. Instruments may be plucked, bowed, struck, or blown.

A good listener can identify an instrument by its special sound, called **timber** (tăm′ bər). Musical groups can also be identified by their special timbre.

A **band** is made up of people who play instruments that are blown or struck.

An **orchestra** has many of the same instruments as the band, along with many stringed instruments.

16

A **choir** is a group of people who use their voices to make music. Men's voices usually sound lower than women's voices.

In a children's choir, boys and girls use their voices to make music. There is not much difference between the timbres of boys' and girls' voices.

Bands, orchestras, and choirs can all make beautiful music. Each group has its own special timbre.

America

My country, 'tis of thee,
Sweet land of liberty,
Of thee I sing.
Land where my fathers died,
Land of the pilgrims' pride,
From every mountainside
Let freedom ring.

Our fathers' God, to Thee,
Author of liberty,
To Thee we sing.
Long may our land be bright
With freedom's holy light;
Protect us by Thy might,
Great God, our King.

O Make a Joyful Noise

The Bible says Jubal of old
Two instruments did play;
And he became the father of
All those who play today.

Refrain:
O make a joyful noise to God,
Play skillfully for Him;
O make a joyful noise to God,
To praise His holy name.

The Bible says that Miriam,
A timbrel in her hand,
Praised God who took His
   people through
The Red Sea to dry land.

18

The Bible says King Saul would
   cry,
"Let David come to me."
Then David played his harp
   and made
The evil spirit flee.

The Bible says that Joshua
Told seven priests to blow
Their trumpets, and the walls
   would fall
Around old Jericho.

The Bible says the Levites played
Their cymbals just to show
That as they sang and praised the
   Lord,
Their temple walls would grow.

Johnny Schmoker

Johnny Schmoker,
Johnny Schmoker,
Can you sing, can you play?
I can play upon my horn.

Johnny Schmoker,
Johnny Schmoker,
Can you sing, can you play?
I can play upon my oboe.

Johnny Schmoker,
Johnny Schmoker,
Can you sing, can you play?
I can play on my bassoon.

Johnny Schmoker,
Johnny Schmoker,
Can you sing, can you play?
I can play on my viola.

21

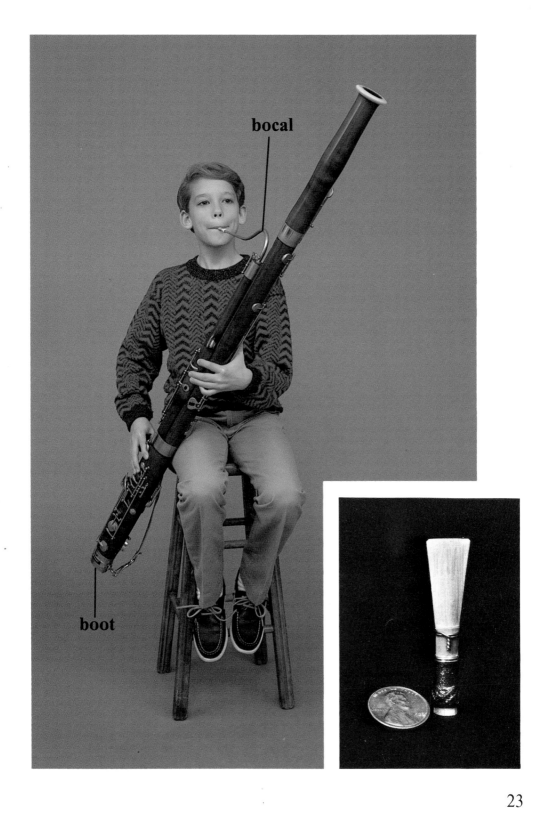

bocal

boot

Morning

from *Peer Gynt Suite No. 1*

by Edvard Grieg

The flute plays the melody as "Morning" begins. Listen for the oboe, the string instruments, the cello, the trumpets, the horns, the clarinet and the bassoon as they play the melody. Point to the pictures as you listen.

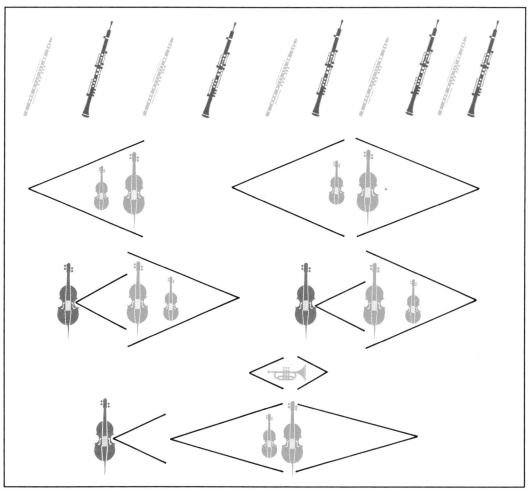

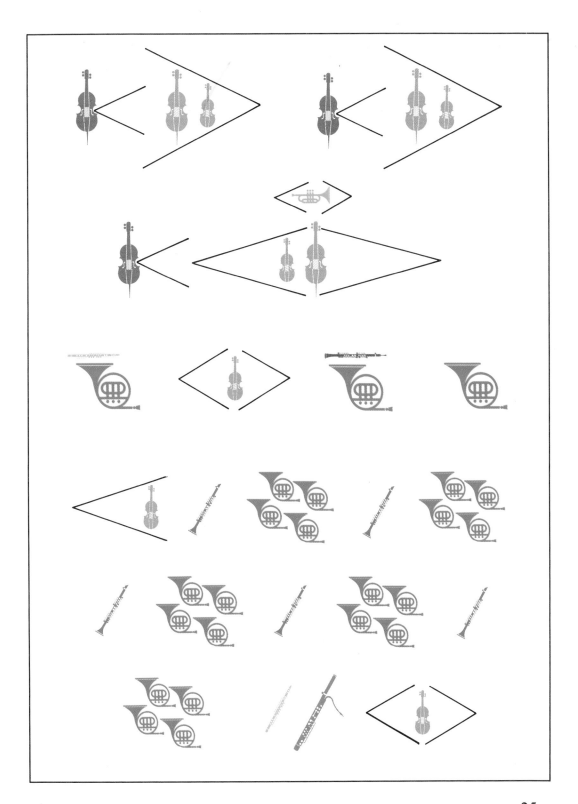

Edvard Grieg

Young Edvard Grieg did not want to be a composer, and he did not like to practice the piano. But Edvard's mother did not want a lazy son, so she made Edvard practice every day. When he became a fine pianist, Edvard could see that his mother knew what was best.

Edvard Grieg lived in the beautiful land of Norway. Close your eyes and listen to Grieg's song called "Morning." What does the music make you see? Think of the sun rising over a tall, snowy mountain. Maybe you see little birds stretching their wings to greet the new day. Grieg saw these things in Norway, and he tried to show them in his music.

Grieg wrote songs in a tiny hut by the sea. People from the town would walk to the hut to hear Grieg's music, but Grieg did not want the people to listen to him. One day when he asked some men to help him move, they just picked up the hut and moved it high up on a cliff. Grieg wanted to thank the men so he played some songs for them. He was happy on the cliff because there he could be alone at last to write his music.

Steps and Leaps

Melodies can move by steps, or by leaps, or by both steps and leaps.

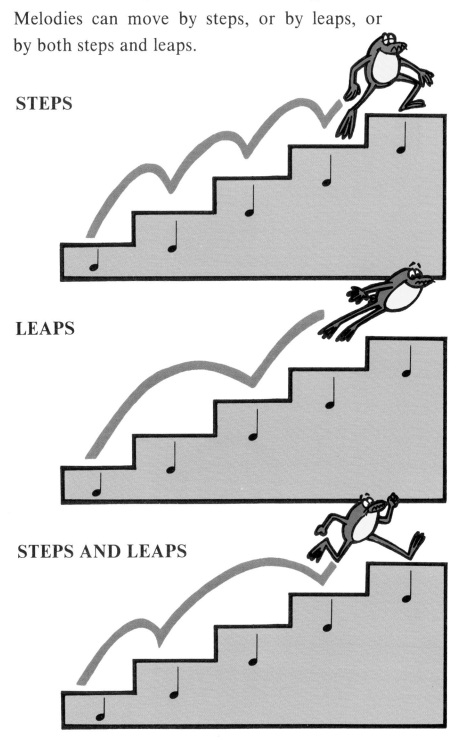

STEPS

LEAPS

STEPS AND LEAPS

Praise Him, Praise Him

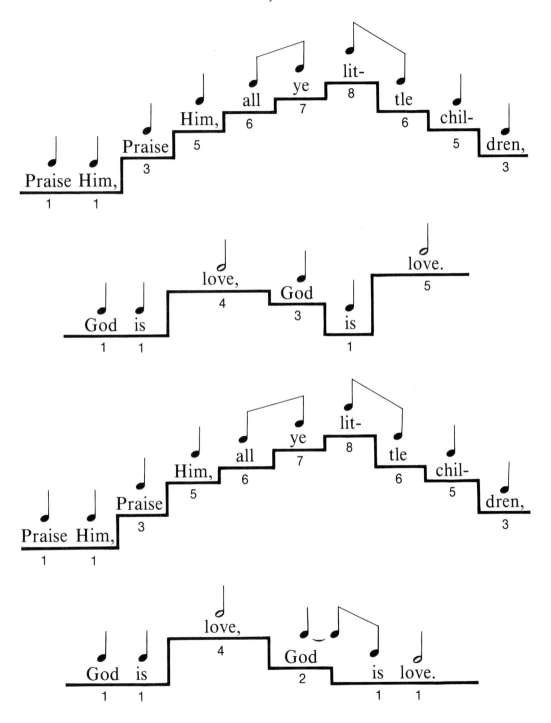

Peter and the Wolf

by Sergei Prokofiev

Before the storyteller begins our tale, he wants to make sure that you know everybody in the story, so he is going to give you a quiz. Do you think that you can get a perfect score?

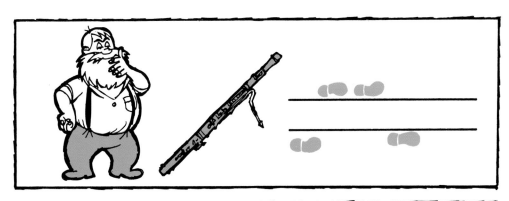

Peter and the Wolf

Peter and the Wolf

Reading Reminders

These are notes. They tell us the rhythm of the music.

When we see notes high and low, we can read the shape of the melody.

When notes are arranged on a line or group of lines called a **staff,** we can read the exact pitches of our melody.

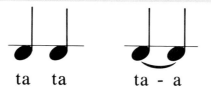

ta   ta   ta - a

When two notes on the same pitch are hooked together with a curved line, we call the line a **tie.**

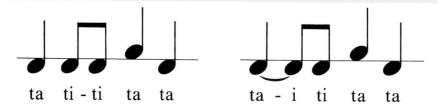

ta ti - ti ta ta   ta - i ti ta ta

Come, Ye Thankful People, Come

Over the River and Through the Wood

O-ver the riv-er and through the wood,
s   s   s   s   m
To Grandfather's house we go;

The horse knows the way to carry the sleigh,

Through the white and drifted snow.

O-ver the riv-er and through the wood,
s   s   s   s   m
Oh, how the wind does blow!

It stings the toes and bites the nose,

As over the ground we go.

Polly Wolly Doodle

U. S. Folk Song

d   r   m   m   d   d   r   m m   d

Oh, I went down South for to see my Sal,

Sing Polly wolly doodle all the day.

My Sal she is a spunky gal,

Sing Polly wolly doodle all the day.

d   r   m   d   r   m

Fare thee well, fare thee well,

Fare thee well my fairy fay;

For I'm goin' to Louisiana,

For to meet my Susanna,

Sing Polly wolly doodle all the day.

do   re   mi

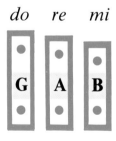

The G bell is our home tone.

Can you play the notes for the shaded words on the bells?

39

Every song has a **home tone.** The home tone is usually the last pitch of a song. When you come to the home tone, the song often sounds finished; the melody sounds as if it has come home.

In singing, we can use hand signs and special syllables, like *do, re,* and *mi.*

Mi is one step higher than *re.*

Re is one step higher than *do.*

Do is the home tone.

When you listen to music, you can sense two different rhythms.

The steady, even rhythm in a song is called the **pulse.** Play the pulse on a hand drum.

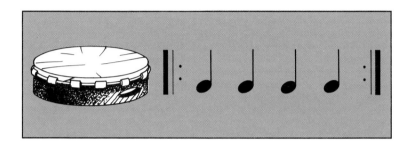

The rhythm that the words make is called the **melodic rhythm.** To play the melodic rhythm, tap the rhythm sticks for each syllable of the words you sing.

Oats, Peas, Beans

m   m   m   r   d   d   d

Oats, peas, beans, and barley grow;

Oats, peas, beans, and barley grow;
Do you or I or anyone know
How oats, peas, beans, and barley grow?

First the farmer sows his seed
Then he stands and takes his ease;
He stamps his foot and claps his hands,
And turns around to view his lands.

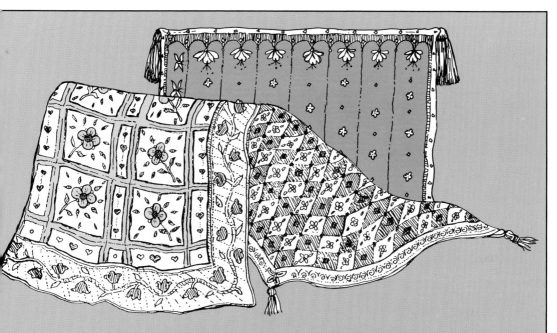

Can you see patterns that repeat in these pictures? Lines, shapes, and colors can form patterns.

You can also find patterns that repeat in music. The rhythm, melody, and harmony can make these repeated patterns.

Most songs have repeated rhythm patterns. These patterns may be even or uneven.

even ▬▬ ▬▬ ▬ ▬ ▬

uneven ▬ ▬ ▪ ▬ ▪ ▬ ▬ ▪

Is "Oats, Peas, Beans" even or uneven?

Using Solfege

When we sing with special words like *do, re, mi,* and *so,* we are using **solfege** (sōl′ fezh). Solfege helps us to listen more carefully and match our pitches better.

so

Using hand signs for our solfege words helps us to remember which pitches are high and which pitches are low.

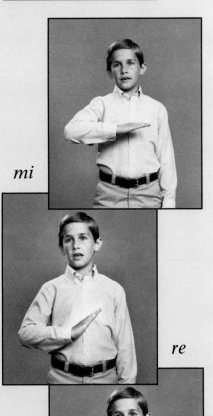

mi

re

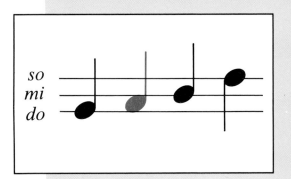

We can also read solfege from a staff. The red note (higher than *do,* lower than *mi*) is *re.*

do

Who's That?

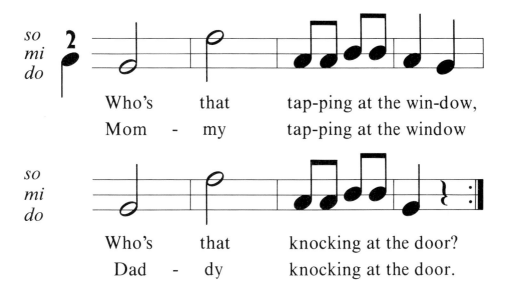

so mi do

Who's   that   tap-ping at the win-dow,
Mom - my   tap-ping at the window

so mi do

Who's   that   knocking at the door?
Dad - dy   knocking at the door.

Always sing words clearly. Don't sing

Instead, sing like this:

Sing the final **s** right before
you sing the next word.

Deedle Deedle Dumpling

Dee-dle dee-dle dump-ling, my son John,

Went to bed with his stock-ings on.

One shoe off and one shoe on,

Dee-dle dee-dle dump-ling, my son John.

What Way Is Best?

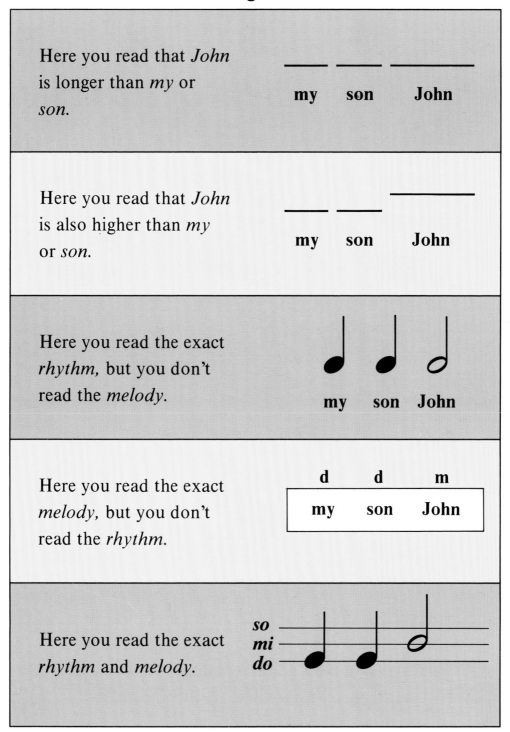

Here you read that *John* is longer than *my* or *son*.

    my   son   John

Here you read that *John* is also higher than *my* or *son*.

    my   son   John

Here you read the exact *rhythm,* but you don't read the *melody.*

    my   son   John

Here you read the exact *melody,* but you don't read the *rhythm.*

    d   d   m
    my   son   John

Here you read the exact *rhythm* and *melody.*

so
mi
do

47

A Five-Note Scale

do   re   mi   so   la

C   D   E   G   A

A **scale** is made up of the pitches found in a song. The pitches are arranged in order from the lowest to the highest. A scale with five pitches is called a **pentatonic scale.** (*Penta* means "five"; *tonic* means "tones" or "notes.")

Here Comes a Bluebird

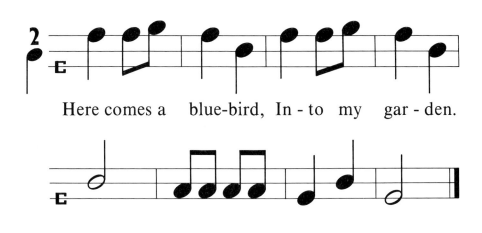

Here comes a blue-bird, In - to my gar - den.

Hi __ did-dle-um-a - day - day - day.

⊏ is the ***do* clef** sign. It tells you where ***do*** is.

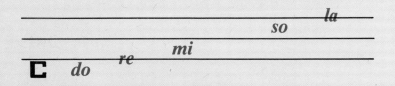

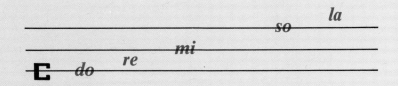

The ***do* clef** sign can move. It can be on any line or space on a staff.

Nothing But the Blood

Robert Lowry

What can wash a-way my sin?
What can make me whole a-gain? Noth-ing but the blood of Je-sus.

Oh! pre-cious is the flow That makes me white as snow;

No oth-er fount I know, Noth-ing but the blood of Je-sus.

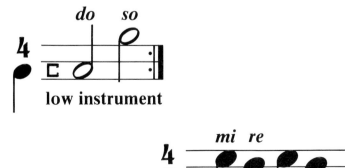

low instrument

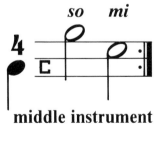

middle instrument

high instrument

51

Adding a New Note

Low la is your new note. You write *la,* to show that this pitch sounds lower than the *la* you have already learned.

When *do* is on a line, *la,* will be on the line below *do*.

do   **la,**

When *do* is on a space, *la,* will be on the space below *do*.

do   **la,**

If *do* is on the bottom line of the staff, *la,* has to be on an added line called a *ledger line*.

do   **la,**

We can also add another line to the staff. A staff can have any number of lines. Most have five lines.

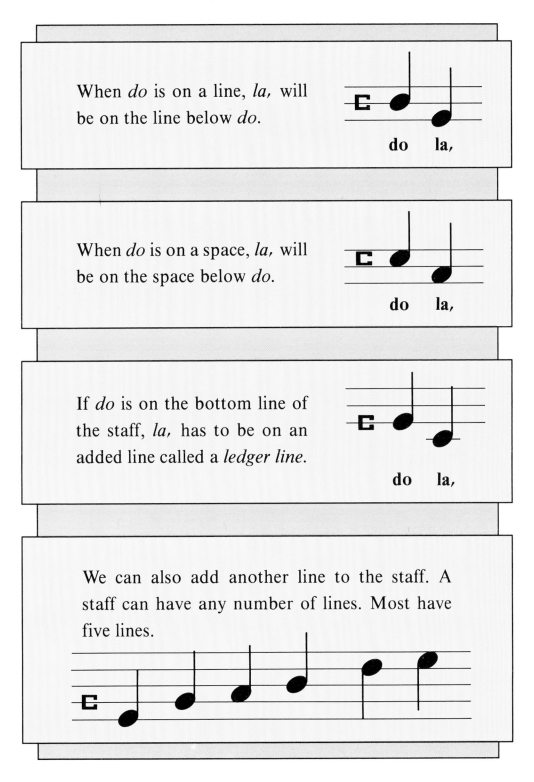

Land of the Silver Birch

Canadian Indian

Land of the sil-ver birch, home of the beav - er,

Where still the might-y moose wan-ders at will,

Blue lake and rock-y shore, I will re - turn once more,

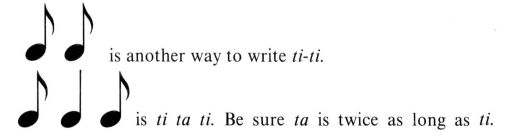

Hi-yah, hi-yah, hi-yah, hi-yah, hi-yah, hi-yah, ho.

is another way to write *ti-ti*.

is *ti ta ti*. Be sure *ta* is twice as long as *ti*.

54

Cumberland Gap

U.S. Folk Song

Help me hunt for *do*. He keeps landing on different lines and spaces

I laid down, Took a lit - tle nap

For - ty one miles from Cum - ber - land Gap.

Cum - ber - land Gap with its cliffs and rocks,

Home of the pan - ther, bear, and fox.

Jennie Jenkins

Will you wear white, O my dear, O my dear? O

will you wear white, Jen-nie Jen - kins? I

won't wear white for the col-or's too bright. I'll

buy me a fol-de- rol-dy til-de-tol-dy, Seek a dou-ble

roll, Jen-nie Jen-kins, roll.

This is the scale for the song, "Jennie Jenkins." Can you sing and sign it?

so,   la,   do   re   mi   so   la

Low *so (so,)* is a step lower than *la,*. It is an octave (eight lines and spaces) below *so*.

Musical Math Facts

ti + *ti* = *ta*

ta + *ta* = *ta-a* (2 *ta*'s)

ta-a + *ta-a* = *ta-a-a-a* (4 *ta*'s)

ta-a-a-a + *ta* = *ta-a-a-a-a* (5 *ta*'s)

ta-a-a-a + *ta-a* = *ta-a-a-a-a-a* (6 *ta*'s)

The Green Leaves Grew All Around

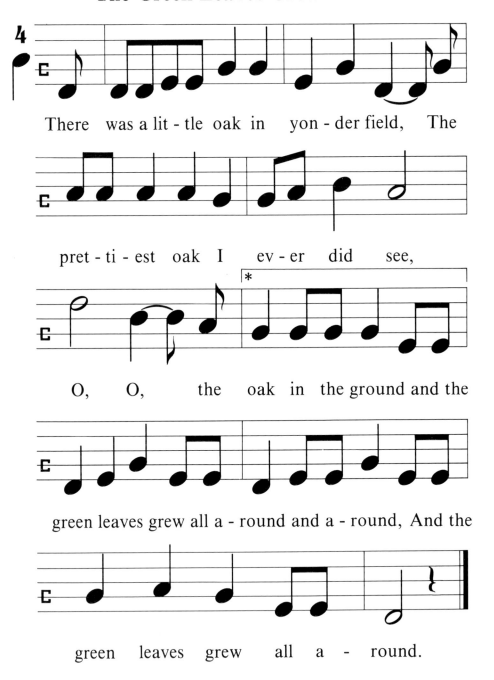

There   was a lit - tle oak in   yon - der field,   The

pret - ti - est oak I   ev - er   did   see,

*

O,   O,   the   oak   in   the ground and the

green leaves grew all a - round and a - round, And the

green   leaves   grew   all   a - round.

*Repeat as needed for other verses.

58

And on that oak there was a limb,
The prettiest limb I ever did see,
O, O, the limb on the oak
And the oak in the ground
And the green leaves grew all around and around,
And the green leaves grew all around.

My Heart

My heart does such wonderful feats;
It isn't a drum, but it beats;
It isn't a brain, but it thinks;
It isn't a boat, but it sinks;
It isn't a singer, but sings;
It isn't a bird, but has wings;
It isn't a frog, but it jumps;
It isn't a rabbit, but thumps;
It isn't asleep, but has dreams;
It isn't a voice, but it screams;
It isn't a dish, but it breaks;
It isn't a tooth, but it aches;
It isn't a tongue, but it tells;
It isn't a wave, but it swells;
It isn't a bird, but it flies;
It isn't a baby, but cries;
It isn't a student, but learns;
It isn't a fire, but it burns;
It isn't a lock, but has keys;
It isn't an eye, but it sees;
So, although, it's my body you see,
It's the HEART of the matter that's me.

Little Wheel A-Turning

U.S. Folk Song

Sing the song, playing the rhythm of the words
in pink on rhythm sticks. A repeated rhythm
is called an **ostinato**.

There's a little wheel a-turning in my heart,

Little wheel a-turning,   little wheel a-turning,

There's a little wheel a-turning in my heart,

Little wheel a-turning,   little wheel a-turning,

In my   heart,   in my heart,

Little wheel a-turning,   little wheel a-turning,

There's a little wheel a-turning in my heart.

Little wheel a-turning,   little wheel a-turning.

The Old Brass Wagon

U.S. Folk Song

This song uses the pentatonic scale. Make up
a special part on the G, A, B, D, and E bells.

1. Circle to the left, the old brass wagon,
   Circle to the left, the old brass wagon,
   Circle to the left, the old brass wagon,
   You're the one my darling.

2. Circle to the right, the old brass wagon, *etc.*

3. Turn yourself around, the old brass wagon, *etc.*

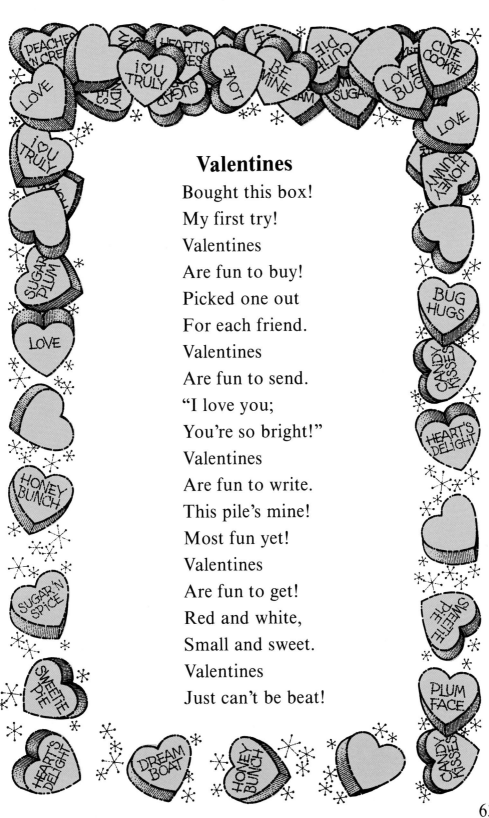

Valentines

Bought this box!
My first try!
Valentines
Are fun to buy!
Picked one out
For each friend.
Valentines
Are fun to send.
"I love you;
You're so bright!"
Valentines
Are fun to write.
This pile's mine!
Most fun yet!
Valentines
Are fun to get!
Red and white,
Small and sweet.
Valentines
Just can't be beat!

Laughing Song

As you read the song, wherever you see a ❪ , think, but do not say or sing, *ta*.

ta   *ta* rest
(think, don't say)

Ha ha ha!— He he he!— An - der - son and Pe - ter - son and

Jen - son and me— Ha ha ha!— He he he!—

Sing - ing all to - geth - er, sing - ing mer - ri - ly.—

Resting Longer

Now read "Laughing Song," making the *ta* rest into a *ta-a* rest. When you see the ▬, think, but do not say or sing the *ta-a*. Some words will be left out.

ta-a   *ta-a* rest

Ha ha!—   He he!—   An-der-son and Pe-ter-son and

Jen-son and—   Ha ha!—   He he—

Sing-ing all to-geth-er sing-ing   mer-ri—

The Changing of the Guard

from *Carmen*

by Georges Bizet

Listen for the fanfare, the A theme, and the B theme.

Theme A:

Theme B:

The Little Shoemaker

Alice Riley   *Jessie Gaynor*

Verse:

man   in a   house
There's a little wee   little   wee

mf

lives
over   the   way   you   see,

window   and   day
sits at the   sews   all

And he

shoes   for   you   and   me.
Making

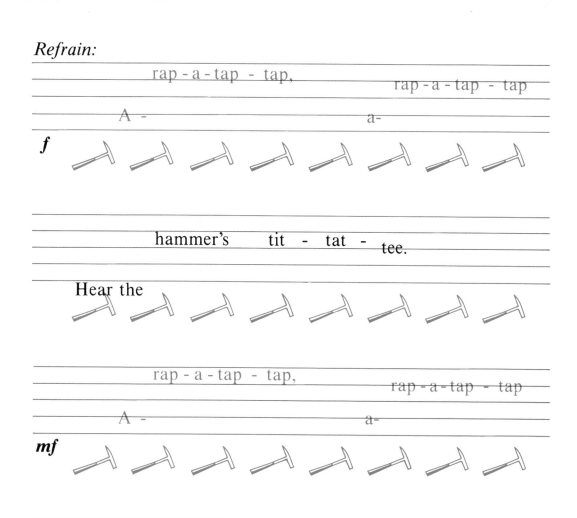

rap - a - tap - tap,   rap - a - tap - tap

A -   a-

f

hammer's   tit - tat - tee.

Hear the

rap - a - tap - tap,   rap - a - tap - tap

A -   a-

mf

shoes   for   you   and   me.

p Making

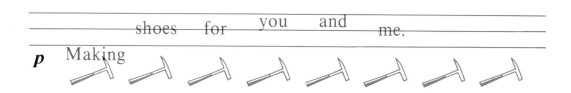

2. He puts his needle in and out,
His thread flies to and fro,
With his tiny awl he bores the holes;
Hear the hammer's busy blow.
Refrain

Nothing But the Blood

Robert Lowry

Verse:

1. What can wash a - way my sin? Noth-ing but the blood of Je - sus;
2. For my par - don this I see, Noth-ing but the blood of Je - sus;

What can make me whole a - gain? Noth-ing but the blood of Je - sus.
For my cleans-ing, this my plea, Noth-ing but the blood of Je - sus.

Refrain:

Oh! pre - cious is the flow That makes me white as snow;

No oth - er fount I know, Noth-ing but the blood of Je - sus.

Same and Different

Good music has parts that are the same and parts that are different.

Which parts of "Nothing But the Blood" are the same? Which are different?

In art you can also find parts that are the same and parts that are different. What shape is repeated in these pictures? Which picture is the most interesting? Why?

Follow the Frog

Follow the music from the beginning to the repeat sign in the first ending.

Jump back to the other repeat sign. Follow the music until you get to the first ending.

Hop over the first ending and follow the music to the double bar, which is the end.

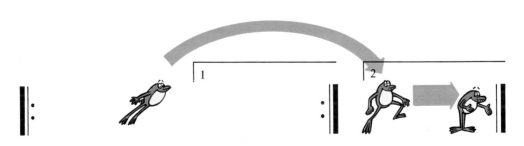

Skip to My Lou

American Folk Song

Fly in the buttermilk, shoo fly shoo!
Fly in the buttermilk, shoo fly shoo!
Fly in the buttermilk, shoo fly shoo!
Skip to my Lou, my darling.

Refrain:

‖: Lou, Lou, skip to my Lou,

1. Lou, Lou, skip to my Lou. :‖

2. Skip to my Lou, my darling. ‖

Staccato ostinato *Play 8 times.*

‖: Skip, skip, skip to my Lou :‖

Legato ostinato *Play 8 times.*

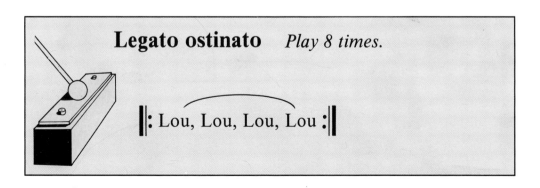

‖: Lou, Lou, Lou, Lou :‖

Ring, Ring the Banjo

Stephen C. Foster

Sing the words. Tap the rhythm pattern lightly
on your desk.

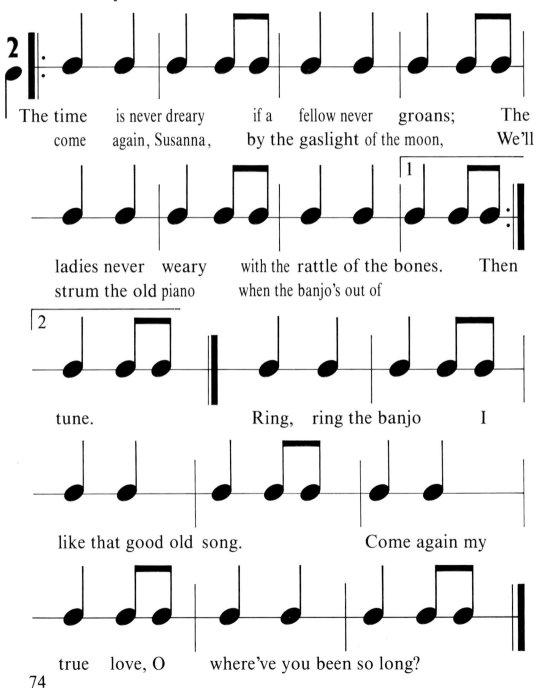

The time   is never dreary   if a   fellow never   groans;   The
come   again, Susanna,   by the gaslight of the moon,   We'll

ladies never   weary   with the rattle of the bones.   Then
strum the old piano   when the banjo's out of

tune.   Ring,   ring the banjo   I

like that good old song.   Come again my

true   love, O   where've you been so long?

Playing Chords

You can play chords for "Billy Boy" and "Oh, Dear! What Can the Matter Be?" Watch the music carefully to see when the chord changes.

On the Autoharp, press the chord bar down with your finger. Hold a pick in your other hand, and strum across the strings from the lowest to highest.

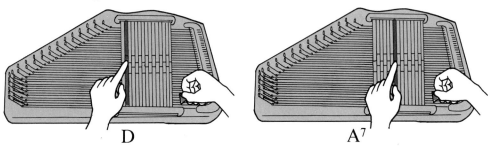

D   A⁷

On the piano, find a group of three keys near the center of the keyboard. Use your fingers to press down the keys that are shown here colored red.

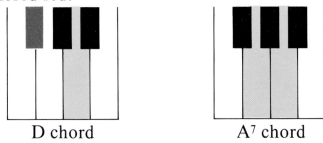

D chord   A⁷ chord

On the bells, play only if your bell belongs in the chord. The *A* bell belongs in both chords.

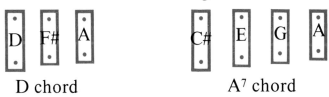

D chord   A⁷ chord

Billy Boy

English Folk Song

Sing "Billy Boy," playing chords on the
Autoharp.

D

1. Oh, where have you been, Billy
2. Can she make a cherry pie, Billy

Boy, Billy Boy? Oh, where have you been, charming
Boy, Billy Boy? Can she make a cherry pie, charming

A⁷

Billy? I have been to see my wife, she's the
Billy? She can make a cherry pie, quick's a

D    A⁷

joy of my life; she's a young thing and cannot
cat can wink her eye; she's a young thing and cannot

D

leave her mother.
leave her mother.

77

Oh, Dear, What Can the Matter Be?

English Folk Song

Play chords on the words in blue. Change chords
when the letter above the words changes.

D

Oh, dear! What can the matter be?

A⁷

Dear, dear! What can the matter be?

D

Oh, dear! What can the matter be?

A⁷   D

Johnny's so long at the fair.

fine*

*fine (fē′ nā) is Italian for "finish."

D
He promised to bring me a basket of posies

A⁷
A garland of lilies, a garland of roses,

D
He promised to bring me a bunch of blue ribbons

A⁷   D
To tie up my bonnie brown hair

da capo*

*****da capo** (dä cä′ pō) is Italian for "go back to the beginning."

People and Music

Some people study music for many years. They may play an instrument, sing, or write music very well. A person who writes music for a living is called a **composer**. Franz Schubert was a composer who wrote many songs that we enjoy today.

Franz Schubert

The Linden Tree

from Winter Journey   *by Franz Schubert*

By the well before the doorway
There stands a linden tree.
How often in its shadow
Sweet thoughts have come to me.
I played upon its branches
And rested in its shade.
In joy alike and sadness,
The tree a shelter made.

A good composer often repeats short melody patterns within a song. The pink and yellow lines show places where Schubert repeats a melody in "The Linden Tree."

Listen to "March Militaire" by Schubert.
Can you hear any repeated patterns?

Shoo, Fly, Don't Bother Me

Billy Reeves   *Frank Campbell*

Find the repeated melody and rhythm patterns
in this song.

Refrain   Shoo, fly, don't bother me,
Shoo, fly, don't bother me,
Shoo, fly, don't bother me,
For I belong to somebody.

Verse   I feel, I feel, I feel,
I feel like a morning star,
I feel, I feel, I feel,
I feel like a morning star.

Sing refrain again.

All people can enjoy making music. Some people sing songs as they work. Others sing or whistle a tune to pass the time of day. Children often sing songs while they're playing.

The song "Shoo, Fly, Don't Bother Me" may have been made up by people who worked making sugar. As they stirred barrels of a thick brown syrup called molasses, flies swarmed around them. Singing this cheerful song probably helped to make their hard work seem easier.

Someone finally wrote down the words and music to the song. Soon many people were singing the "Shoo Fly" song. Soldiers during the War Between the States sang it as they marched. Children sang it as they played. Families who moved to the new lands in the West sang it as they traveled in wagon trains.

Sometimes people work together to write music. One person writes the words, and the other person writes or chooses music to fit the words.

John Newton wrote the words to the hymn "Amazing Grace." The words tell how God saved him from his sinful life as a slave trader. The music to "Amazing Grace" is an American melody by an unknown composer.

Amazing Grace

John Newton   *American Melody*

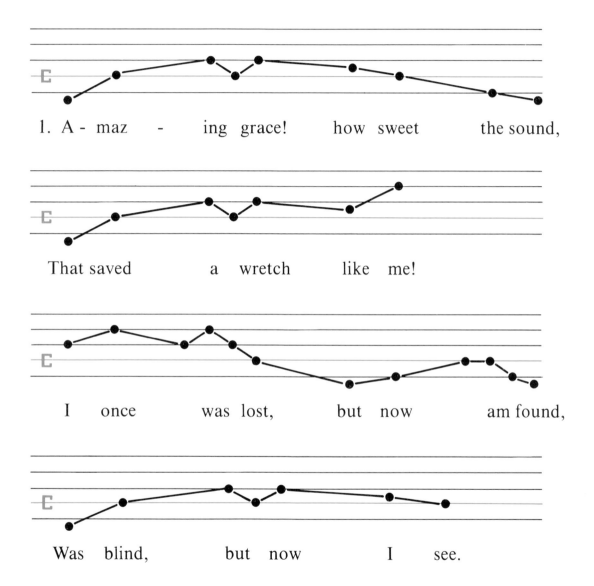

1. A - maz - ing grace! how sweet the sound,

That saved a wretch like me!

I once was lost, but now am found,

Was blind, but now I see.

Some people make their living by singing or by playing music. Ira Sankey led the singing for a famous preacher, Dwight L. Moody. Just before Mr. Moody came to speak, Mr. Sankey would often sing a solo or lead the choir in a special song. Ira Sankey also wrote music for gospel songs and hymns. One of his best-loved songs is "A Shelter in the Time of Storm."

A Shelter in the Time of Storm

Vernon Charlesworth   *Ira Sankey*

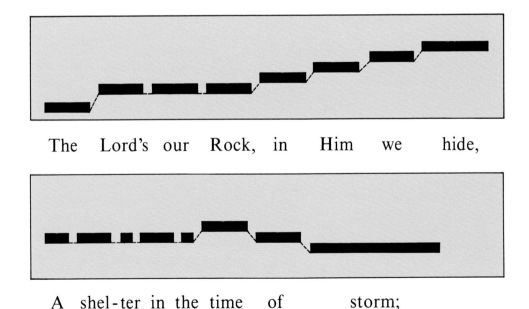

The   Lord's   our   Rock,   in   Him   we   hide,

A   shel-ter   in   the   time   of   storm;

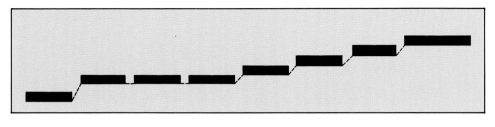

Se - cure what - ev - er ill be - tide,

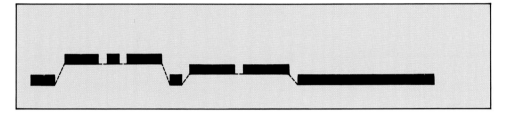

A shel-ter in the time of storm.

Refrain Oh, Jesus is a rock in a weary land,
A weary land, a weary land;
Oh, Jesus is a rock in a weary land,
A shelter in the time of storm.

How Music Is Made

Songs blend music and words. A songwriter often writes the words first. He then chooses or composes a melody that seems to fit the words.

The notes in a melody move up and down. Sometimes a note repeats. When a melody moves, it moves by a step or a leap.

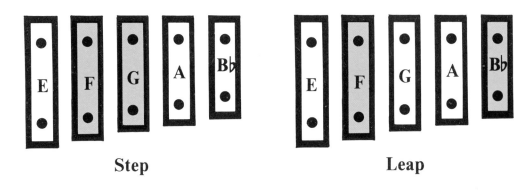

Step   **Leap**

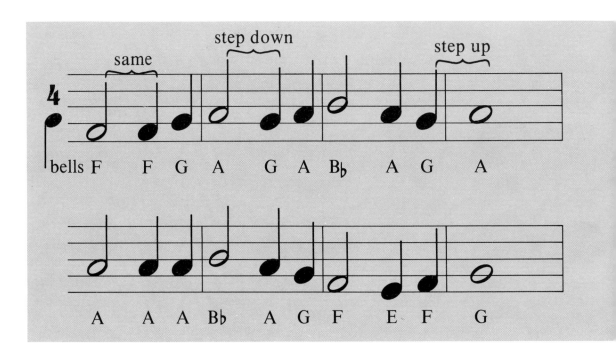

When I Survey

Isaac Watts

When I survey the wondrous cross,

On which the Prince of glory died,

My richest gain I count but loss,

And pour contempt on all my pride.

Play the melody to "When I Survey" on the bells.

Does the melody fit the words?

Does the melody move by steps or leaps?

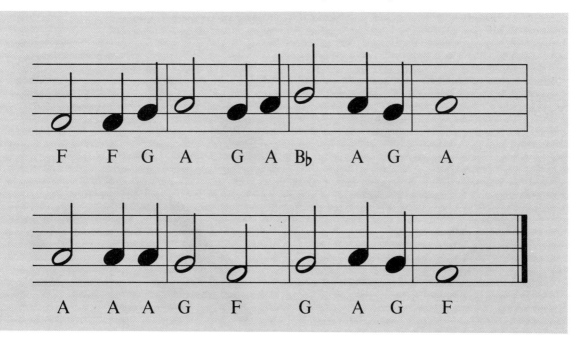

F F G A G A B♭ A G A

A A A G F G A G F

Hallelujah, What a Saviour!

Philip P. Bliss   *Philip P. Bliss*

Philip P. Bliss wrote both the words and music to "Hallelujah, What a Saviour!" This song is often sung at Easter. Can you find the steps and leaps?

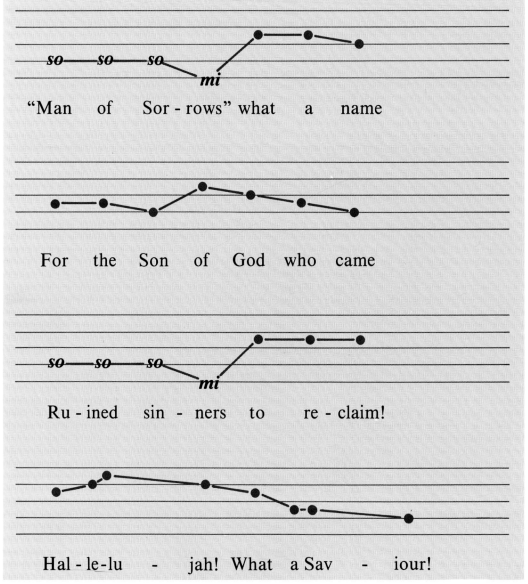

so so so
mi

"Man   of   Sor - rows" what   a   name

For   the   Son   of   God   who   came

so so so
mi

Ru - ined   sin - ners   to   re - claim!

Hal - le-lu   -   jah! What a Sav   -   iour!

Lifted up was He to die
"It is finished," was His cry;
Now in heav'n exalted high;
Hallelujah! What a Saviour!

When He comes, our glorious King,
All His ransomed home to bring,
Then anew this song we'll sing:
Hallelujah! What a Saviour!

Changing Tempo

Composers often give us special instructions so that we can better express their feelings and ideas about the music. Some instructions tell us how loudly or softly to play or sing. Other instructions tell us how quickly or slowly to perform the music.

A train starts out slowly from its station. Little by little, the engine gains in speed. It chugs steadily down the track for many miles. As another station comes into view, the brakeman puts on the brake. Slower, slower go the wheels until the train stops at last.

Get On Board

Spiritual

Start slow, then accel.

Get on board, little children,
Get on board, little children,
Get on board, little children,
There's room for many a-more.

Steady, bright tempo

The gospel train's a-coming,
I hear it just at hand,
I hear the car wheels rumbling
And rolling through the land.

rit. little by little

Get on board, little children,
Get on board, little children,
Get on board, little children,
There's room for many a-more.

Singing with Expression

Before singing a song, look at the words and melody. Think about the mood, feeling, and message that the song expresses.

Ah, Poor Bird

English Folk Song

1. Ah,   poor   bird,   you   must   fly

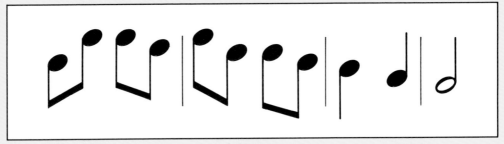

To a warm - er cli - mate and a   blu - er   sky.

2. In the spring,
   Here I'll be,
   And you will come back again
   to sing for me.

When you sing this song, should it be fast or slow? Should it be loud or soft? Should you have a happy voice or a rather sad voice?

Crocodile Song

Traditional

Oh, she 🚢 away on a ☀️ summer day

On the back of a 🐊

"You see," said 👧, "he's as tame as he can 🐝.

I'll ride 🐊 down the 🏝,

Find the sections that have the same melody.
What color are they?

The [alligator] winked his [eye] as she bade them all [waving girl],

Wearing a happy [smile].

At [The End], of the ride, the [girl] was inside,

And the [smile] was on the [alligator]!

Building Blocks of Music

A **pattern** is a short word group, melody, or rhythm that happens several times in a piece of music.

A **phrase** is a more complete musical idea. It often has one or more patterns in it.

A **section** is a group of two or more phrases. It forms a large part of a piece, such as a verse or a refrain.

Can you find examples of a **pattern,** a **phrase,** and a **section** in the song on the next page?

Wonderful Words of Life

Philip P. Bliss   *Philip P. Bliss*

Verse   Sing them over again to me,
          Wonderful words of life;
          Let me more of their beauty see,
          Wonderful words of life.
          Words of life and beauty,
          Teach me faith and duty:

Refrain Beautiful words, wonderful words,
           Wonderful words of life;
           Beautiful words, wonderful words,
           Wonderful words of life.

The Big Parade

Here comes the band in the big pa - rade!

Trum - pets sound! Cym - bals crash! Flags and ban - ner lead the way as

O - boes, pic - co - los tril - ly dil - ly doo - dle,

Rim tick-y tim tick-y ta ta too-dle.

Here comes the band in the big pa-rade!

Sleep, Baby, Sleep

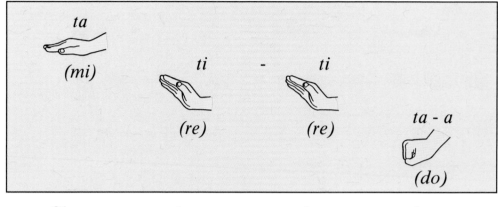

Sleep,   ba - by,   sleep;

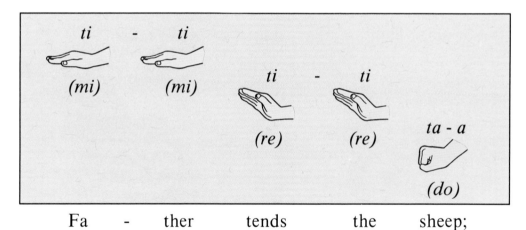

Fa - ther   tends   the   sheep;

Moth - er shakes   the   dream - land   tree and

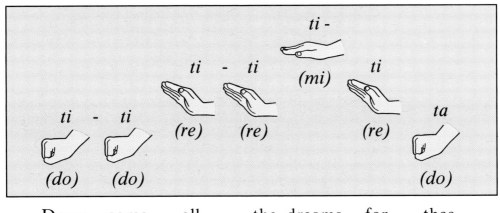

Down   come   all   the dreams   for   thee.

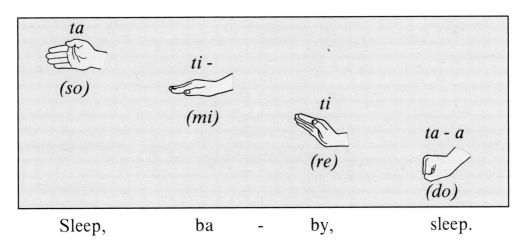

Sleep,   ba - by,   sleep.

Can you write the rhythm of this song using ♩ , ♫ , and ♩ ?

Can you write the melody of this song using a five-line staff?

Style in the Arts: Old and New

Jan Molenaer, *Children Making Music.* The National Gallery, London

Roger Bruckner,
Composition Number Three

Styles in music and art change as the years go by. Composers and artists discover new ways to express their ideas.

Joseph Haydn was born 150 years before Zoltán Kodály. Both men composed music about clocks. Listen to the way each composer uses melody, harmony, rhythm, and timbre. How are these two pieces different?

An artist uses line, shape, color, and space in creating a work of art. Look carefully at the paintings on pages 104 and 105. How are they different?

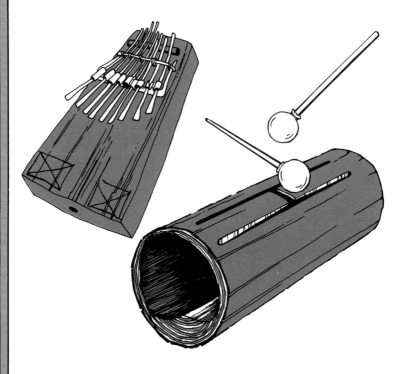

The **obodom** (slit drum) is made from a hollow log. People send messages through the jungle by playing special rhythm and melody patterns on the drum.

The **mbira** (thumb piano) is made from a wooden box or hollow gourd. Many pieces of metal are connected to it. To pass the time, travelers play mbiras as they walk from village to village.

Kokoleoko*

(The Rooster's Call)

This song about the rooster has the simple melody and lively rhythm that many African folk songs have.

Kokoleoko, Mama, kokoleoko,
Kokoleoko, chicken crowing for day.

Aby*, Sarah, aby,
Aby, chicken crowing for day.

***Kokoleoko** is the African version of cock-a-doodle-doo.

***Aby** means good-bye.

An African Drum Piece

Set a steady tempo by counting to eight over and over again. Play your instrument only on the green numbers. Rest (do not play, but keep counting) on the black numbers.

The Genius of the Piano

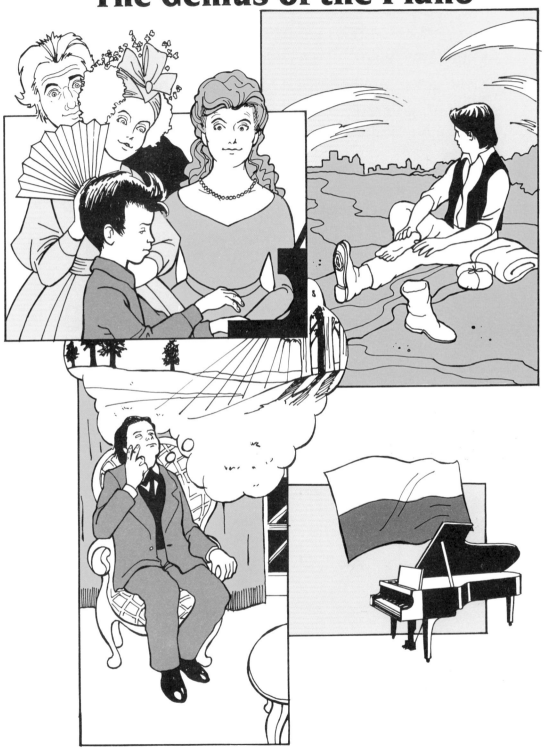

Have you ever wondered how a piano makes its sound? When someone strikes a piano key, a hammer inside the piano hits several strings. The strings move back and forth very quickly. Because they are stretched tightly over a sounding board, the movement of the strings makes a beautiful sound.

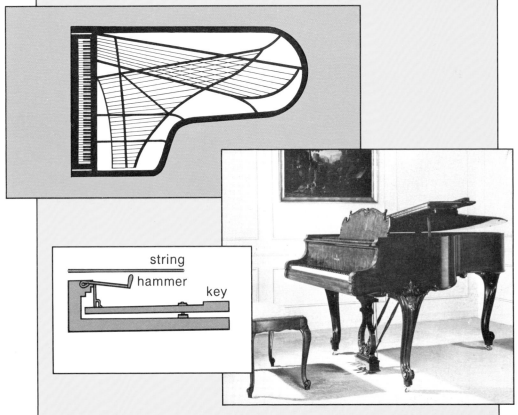

Look for the strings in the picture of the grand piano. The low piano keys have the longest strings, and the high piano keys have the shortest strings.

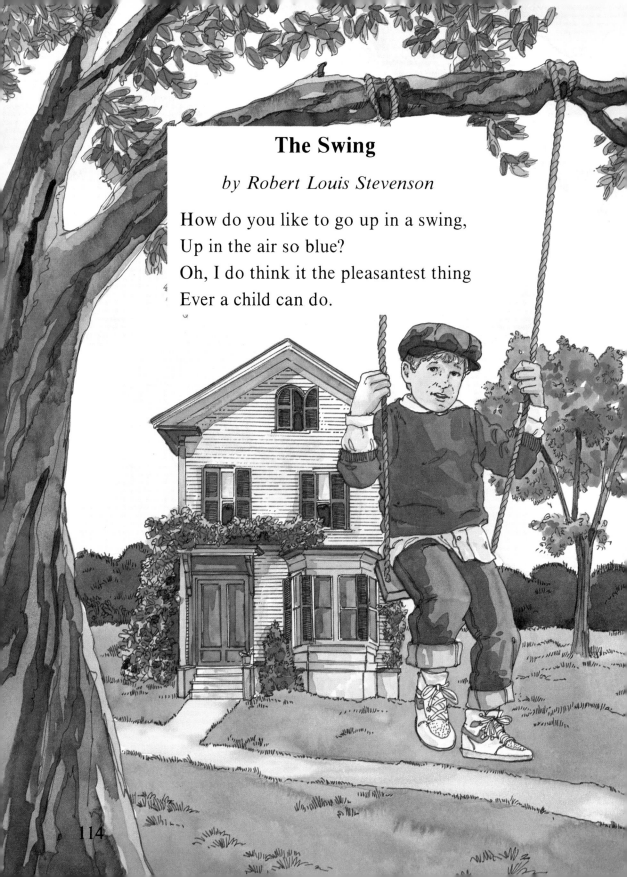

The Swing

by Robert Louis Stevenson

How do you like to go up in a swing,
Up in the air so blue?
Oh, I do think it the pleasantest thing
Ever a child can do.

Make Your Own Song

1. Say the poem until you know it well.

2. Make up a melody for the first line. Sing it several times.

3. Make up a different melody for the second line and sing it several times.

4. For the third line of the poem, use the same melody you made up for the first line.

5. The last line can have the same melody as the second line, or you could make up a new melody. End on the home tone.

6. Sing the whole song several times, and then write it down so that you will remember it.

7. Make your song more musical by adding dynamics.

Choosing Good Music

Whether therefore ye eat, or drink, or whatsoever ye do, do all to the glory of God.

I Corinthians 10:31

The Bible tells us to do everything to God's glory. The music we enjoy should be pleasing to God, whether it is **sacred** or **secular.**

When you sing a sacred song, look at the words. Be sure that they agree with what the Bible says.

Before you sing a secular song, be sure that the words encourage you to do things that are right and to think about things that are good.

I Think When I Read That Sweet Story

Jemima Luke   *Joan Pinkston*

I think when I read that sweet story of old,
When Jesus was here among men;
How He called little children like lambs to His fold.
I should like to have been with Him then!
I wish that His hands had been placed on my head,
That His arms had been thrown around me,
And that I might have seen His kind look when He said,
"Let the little ones come unto me."

Both this painting and the song on the next page teach us that God is powerful. They also remind us that God made everything. These are works that reflect the greatness of God.

Is God reflected in the **way** the artist painted his picture? Does his use of line and shape help us to see God's power?

Cristoforo Scacco, *God the Father*. Bob Jones University Collection of Sacred Art

I Sing the Mighty Power of God

Isaac Watts   *Herzogl Songbook, 1784*

I sing the mighty pow'r of God
That made the mountains rise,
That spread the flowing seas abroad
And built the lofty skies.
I sing the wisdom that ordained
The sun to rule by day;
The moon shines full at His command
And all the stars obey.

Is God reflected in the **way** the composer wrote this song? Do the melody, harmony, and rhythm fit the meaning of the words?

Redeemed

Fanny Crosby   *William Kirkpatrick*

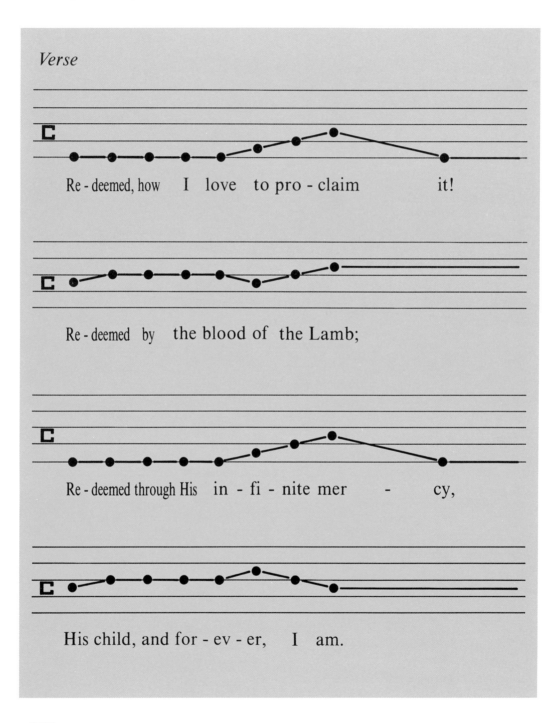

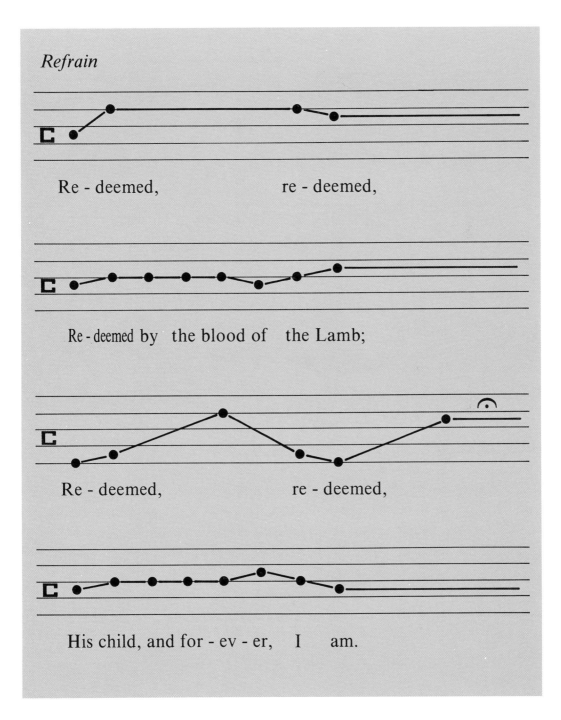

For, lo, the winter is past,
The rain is over and gone;
The flowers appear on the earth;
The time of the singing of birds is come,
And the voice of the turtle* is heard in our land.

Song of Solomon 2:11-12

*turtledove

Song Index

Listening Index